# LADY ANNE
## A Chronicle in Verse

*by*
## ANTJIE KROG

*Translated from the Afrikaans and with a Preface by the Poet*

Bucknell University Press

Published by Bucknell University Press
Co-published with The Rowman & Littlefield Publishing Group, Inc.
4501 Forbes Boulevard, Suite 200, Lanham, Maryland 20706
www.rowman.com

Unit A, Whitacre Mews, 26-34 Stannary Street, London SE11 4AB, United Kingdom

Copyright ©2017 A.E. Samuel
Published by agreement with NB Publishers, a division of Media24 Boeke (Pty) Ltd.
Originally published by Taurus in 1989 and subsequently in 2004 by Human & Rousseau, an imprint of NB Publishers

*All rights reserved.* No part of this book may be reproduced in any form or by any electronic or mechanical means, including information storage and retrieval systems, without written permission from the publisher, except by a reviewer who may quote passages in a review.

British Library Cataloguing in Publication Information Available

Library of Congress Cataloging-in-Publication Data Available
**Library of Congress Control Number: 2016955282**
ISBN 978-1-61148-815-9 (cloth: alk. paper)
ISBN 978-1-61148-816-6 (elec)

∞™ The paper used in this publication meets the minimum requirements of American National Standard for Information Sciences – Permanence of Paper for Printed Library Materials, ANSI/NISO Z39.48-1992.

Printed in the United States of America

Frontispiece: *Lady Anne Barnard* by Richard Cosway RA (1742-1821). Miniature on ivory, 5.7 x 4.6 cm. William Fehr Collection, Cape Town. Reproduced by permission of Africa Media Online.

# Contents

ACKNOWLEDGEMENTS . . . . . . . . . . . . . . . . . . . . . . . . . . . . . . . . . VII
PREFACE . . . . . . . . . . . . . . . . . . . . . . . . . . . . . . . . . . . . . . . . . . . . . . IX

PART I . . . . . . . . . . . . . . . . . . . . . . . . . . . . . . . . . . . . . . . . . . . . . . . . 1
On board Sir Edward Hughes 23rd Feb. – 1797
2.30 South latitude / 17 West longitude / 9th Mar. – 1797
The Country of the Lindsays of the Byres
(a letter from Fife, 1300, writer unknown)
Song written before the birth of Lady Anne Lindsay (1750)
"two years next month / since my last poetry volume"
"once more / before an empty page"
Kroonstad March '86
hail Lady Anne Barnard!
Cape of Good Hope 4th May – 1797

PART II . . . . . . . . . . . . . . . . . . . . . . . . . . . . . . . . . . . . . . . . . . . . . . 13
Cape of Good Hope 10th July – 1797
Castle October 1797
Castle 12th Oct. – 1797
Castle 1798
Auld Robin Gray written by Lady Anne Barnard
Gossip from diaries and letters
Old Lady Lindsay from Scotland
To Windham 1st Nov. – 1793
St Wolstans near Dublin 10th Dec. – 1793
Dublin 12th July – 1794
Kroonstad first state of emergency July 1985
first Christmas weekend under the second state of emergency 1988

"because among mine I feel more and more ill at ease"
to have or to be
gnome
parole
cape of good hope
Lady Anne as guide because a hero needs a bard
"I think I am the first" – Lady Anne on Table Mountain

**PART III (V)** ................................................... 37
The Drup Kelder Tuesday 8th May – 1798
Farm of Jakob van Reenen Sunday 13th May – 1798
Monday 14th May – 1798
Tuesday 15th May – 1798
Tuesday 22nd May – 1798
St Andrew's Fife Scotland 25th Aug. – 1987
visit to Balcarres
the ballad of Andries Dundas-Dekker
Genadendal 10th May – 1798
Thursday 31st May – 1798

**PART IV** ......................................................... 55
20th Nov. – 1798
Paradise November 1798
1789
1793
"given line: macho men give me the creeps"
plea to be liberated
"one day my husband feels I do indeed deserve"
slaughtering cattle for the Dutch Reformed Church fête
Lady Anne at the microwave oven
"I smell him young behind the breadcutting machine"
ma will be late

I will always remember
"strategically I do my best"
ballad of the power game
illness
Castle of Good Hope 14th Dec. – 1799
Vineyard 14th May – 1800
Journal ("This sets loose so many images.")
Journal ("empty lies the interior of the land")
Vineyard 16th Feb. – 1801

**PART III (end)** . . . . . . . . . . . . . . . . . . . . . . . . . . . . . . . . . . . . . . . . . . .83
January 1802
new alphabet
transparency of the sole
the heart is the toughest part of the body
Lady Anne Barnard: remembered for her parties in my history book
a poem about guilt
Gothic House Wimbledon 1806
Wimbledon May 1807
Cape of Good Hope June 1807
Cape of Good Hope August 1807
Wimbledon November 1807
Wimbledon 1808
neither family nor friends
epitaph
End
end

**SOURCES** . . . . . . . . . . . . . . . . . . . . . . . . . . . . . . . . . . . . . . . . . . . . .107
**ABOUT THE POET** . . . . . . . . . . . . . . . . . . . . . . . . . . . . . . . . . . . . . .109

# Acknowledgements

Thank you to Greg Clingham who, after stumbling on to the volume *Lady Anne,* thought it worth publishing in English, to Karen Press who generously saved and saved and saved my translation, to Carolyn Forché whose writing guided my first steps into the complexities of writing the political, and to Tony Morphet for being the first reader – he has become, in many ways, the most important benchmark in my writing.

# Preface

*Lady Anne* was published as my seventh volume of poetry in Afrikaans in 1989, a year before the tumultuous upheaval caused by the release of Nelson Mandela and the unbanning of liberation movements. The poems were written during that stressful period of acute black resistance against the apartheid state, suffocating and deadly security police control under a State of Emergency and the detention and deaths of comrades. I was living in a small rural town and teaching in the black townships which one could only enter with special permission.

For many white poets, the eighties presented a crisis. Activists asked: And what did the Afrikaans writers do when Soweto was burning? How can one continue writing about and from an enclosed part of South African society? How was one to write about what was happening in the townships of which one knew only small slices? One dared not pretend that one "knew how it felt" nor tried "to write on behalf of."

I had addressed this challenge in various ways over the years in both my poetry and my life, but by the mid-eighties I wanted to have a solid, in depth and complex confrontation. As nobody of my generation had attempted to use the epic form, I decided to research it and to look for a possible hero. Lady Anne Barnard became my vehicle. I remembered her from my school history book where she was the only woman in the vast gallery of white powerful men. Of her nothing more was said other than that she accompanied her husband and gave big parties at the Castle in Cape Town. I chose her because she represented white privilege and initially frivolousness to me. Research, however, showed her not only as a much more multi-faceted character during the six years she spent at the Cape of Good Hope, but also as a producer of a wealth of letters, diaries and paintings. One of the ironies, of course, was that it was far easier for me to find out things about her than, for instance, about the jailed Nelson Mandela, even to visit places in England and Scotland where she lived. It was easier to access her diaries and paintings, than the words and lives of banned liberation leaders. Yet the whole epic was written while I was teaching in the heat of resistance politics in the townships and I wanted to find a way in which to present in poetry the unbearable complexity of it all.

In 1797 Lady Anne's husband, Andrew Barnard, was sent to the Cape of Good Hope as Secretary to Lord Macartney, first British governor of the Cape Colony. Barnard was given this post by the Secretary for War and Colonies, Henry Dundas. Lady Anne, who was well connected to both Dundas and the Prince of Wales, accompanied her husband and became the first lady of the Colony in the absence of Lord Macartney's wife. Her letters and diaries are filled with acute observations and assessments of the situations and people she came across in and around the Cape during her period of residence (1797-1802). She also produced hundreds of drawings and paintings of which most are in Balcarres House, her ancestral home in Scotland. I visited the estate as well as that of Dundas's offspring who, in a story stranger than fiction, married an Afrikaner. I sourced several books compiled from her diaries and letters, as well as *Lady Anne Barnard at the Cape of Good Hope* 1797-1802 (1924) by Dorothea Fairbridge who suggests Lady Anne's love for the anti-slavery activist William Windham.

In *Lady Anne* structurally and technically I made use of a range of ideas associated with deconstruction. The solid narrative of the Lady was constantly broken by the voice of the bard/poet torn among many loyalties, texts, discrepancies, biases, pressures, voices, election posters, even a menstruation chart with which the bard tried to avoid pregnancy. The narrative of the Lady was suspect because it had been put together by the praise-singing bard, who in her turn was regularly side-tracked by a world reeling with demands and also politically suspect. So the main narrative consisted of notes from Lady Anne's letters and journals, but also imagined moments. The bard reacted to the telling as well as asserting her own life's complications to signal the complexities of writing, of writing-with-a-purpose, of living in the face of poverty and of the impossible possibility of writing honestly and truly about anything in this Country of Good Hope.

This is done both in content and in form. For example, the five different parts are mis-arranged: the final part becomes part three (in which the Lady could break out of the superficial confinements around her to truly participate in a struggle for justice). But of course she doesn't break out, so the last part (Part III) has to have two endings: one by the Lady claiming that she is just one text/voice among many and these texts will in their turn embrace or reject her shortcomings. The ending by the bard is more merciless:

> but the most important part of this bankrupt poem
> is its farewell to you (hear the gong at the gallows)
> and your kind
> and your kind's language
> from now on you will have to dither elsewhere
>
> under my thumb lies the delicate syntax of your throat.

You and your language, the specific syntax of privilege in your throat, is to be stopped by the bard's hand. The bard also knows that "killing" the subject of her poetry means the end of the bard herself.

The volume did well and received the highest award in Afrikaans literature for poetry. However, after the release of Mandela the following year and the new era of openness, reconciliation and an emphasis on the suffering of black people under apartheid, I was deeply disappointed in myself that absolutely nothing of what was happening could be detected in the volume. But translating these poems twenty-six years later, I realise that they were busy then with what is now being put under the spotlight by the angry black youth: the many layers of white privilege, the impossibility of adequately responding to guilt as well as to the colonial gaze.

Both the Lady and her Bard have lived their lives without honour – failing the demands of their time.

# LADY ANNE
## ANTJIE KROG

# Part I

Bram Fischer ended his statement to the court in Pretoria, on 28 March 1966, with the words of one of Afrikanerdom's great leaders, President Kruger: *Met vertrouwen leggen wij onze zaak open voor de geheele wereld. Het zij wij overwinnen, het zij wij sterven: de vrijheid zal in Afrika rijzen als de zon uit de morgenwolken.'*

Stockenström's Levebre is a woman undergoing a spiritual crisis common enough in our time and place, a crisis in which the urge to opt for apocalypse and death is almost overwhelming.

"Did he die for the maintenance of our way of life? I mean, for the White way of life, for it is the White people of South Africa who say what the way of life must be."

Zaïre, Kenia, Uganda, Zambië – almal verstrengel en verstrik in die spinnerak van imperialistiese en internasionale kapitalisme, waar die armes armer en die rykes ryker word, waar die lande verdeeld is op grond van stamme, waar daar dikwels militêre ingryping is. Die enigste bestendigheid lê by die groot maatskappye wat die land uitbuit.

His brother Timothy joined the SADF in January 1979 and became a commissioned officer. He also volunteered to serve in northern Namibia and "died 300km inside Angola". "He was painted black and was wearing a Unita uniform," Paton wrote. He died painlessly and fast (one bullet), the family was told. Timothy was given a *pro patria* medal.

Only the poor and oppressed can love universally, only they can truly love the rich and powerful as themselves. Only the love of the poor and oppressed is all-inclusive, whereas the love of the oppressor is exclusive. (...) An oppressor can love the oppressed only if he or she adopts, to the degree to which this is possible, the perspective of the poor, and commits himself or herself to a fundamental change of those structures that keep the poor and oppressed deprived and powerless.

To locate a text without careful attention to the interplay (in the case of Brink) between textual procedure and proposition, is to ignore the constructedness of its concepts, its exercise of power, its complicity with the oppressor; it is to fall into the elaborately set-up trap of the text; of the text as ally, as strategy, as incarnation of a hegemonic régime; in short, it is a failure to transgress.

Dit help nie om 'n opponent só te wil skep wat (as spieëlbeeld) jou eie opsies sal regverdig nie. Daarop bou jy dan jou analises en regverdig of verklaar of verskoon sodoende jou basiese denkfout. Daarom lyk dit vir my asof jou denke nog nie losgekom het uit die wit verf nie.

Groete,
BREYTEN

"As my kinders nie kan leer om wit Afrikane te word nie, vernietig ek hul toekoms," sê dr Smith. (...) "Ek dink hierdie land het 'n revolusie nodig om hom weer gesond te maak."

The grave will render all alike
So, if only in our lifetime, let us be various!
For what reason should we rush from the mansion,

We cannot judge our homeland. The sword of justice
will stick fast in our personal disgrace:
                      Brodsky

**On board Sir Edward Hughes**
**23rd Feb. – 1797**

**To Henry Dundas**

Who *is* it that bloody well sends me downwards
to foreign soils? Above all, why? Fabricated from
an abundance of stains and knobs my Highland origin
always matters to me – stony gaiters and mist,
an intimacy there where water lists
the only reflection – a saddened green
dendrite touch along my tongue:
like you, Sir, I was purified for castles.

On deck under my blanket my senses sting,
I am suspended, grim swine in the rigging
of sound and salt spray; my fingers
fondle blocks of umber,
carmine, a new cinnabar
(marked down by Newmans in London)
to pound this wretched life of yours and mine
into dignity, into blends of poetry and paint.

Suddenly out of the sea, slightly to one side, a parasol of crystal
shimmering over skin. Barnard fires his gun. A jet
of bubbles vibrates thunderously from a spout – will it
surface furiously beneath the ship so that we tumble,
sucked into a vortex with blank-eyed animals, sails billowing
underwater, wobbling deck, cannon snouts pointing upwards
under fleeces of hair (mine a blonde combless fern
or fin) in a ring o'roses slowly sinking to the dregs?

**2.30 South latitude**
**17 West longitude**
**9th Mar. – 1797**

**To Henry Dundas**

Prosperously we sail. Tableau on the sunny side:
clothes, bedding dipped in vinegar, effluvium shrivels.
At 12 precisely our keel slid in algae and seaweed
cuts the meridian. Here, so I've heard, the world plunges
out of its own shadow, everything loses its lining.
Across the blazing deck Barnard walks – crumpled
around his ankles a turbot-like flap clings.

My pen keeps itself busy with nothing grand or miraculous
But every stroke nonetheless accurately brutal –
(therefore nothing of this morning's darkening
of my body – prevailed upon
my spine curves, my thickening skin suddenly grins
my hands flap at the rails: dare
I dolphin-dive backward suicidal
among froth and gods and light corpses of dancers).

During the day Mr Barnard and I anoint a future for ourselves
from maps and books, piece by piece around the southern point.

## The Country of the Lindsays of the Byres
## (a letter from Fife, 1300, writer unknown)

a few mornings ago
the frost sharp the sky wide-stretched
I trekked forth
to the country estate of the Lindsays
the seat of the Earl of Crawford
and Balcarres a name
linked with
magnificent corridors of blood
thus the "Lindsays light and gay"
fought at Otterbourne
1388
letting death beam under the bite
at Dettingen and Fontenoy
of bagpipe and virgin snow

*amidst the haunts of men my clansmen*
*think often on the heathery braes*
*of fair Balcarres' sunward-sloping farms*

## Song written before the birth of Lady Anne Lindsay (1750)

Come workers, come soothsayers,
watercarriers, come weavers,
come let us proclaim the birth of the Lindsay
firstborn: hey doun doun derrie doun

the season is filling with oats
the valleys with heather and hen
to the throne he restores
the Scottish White Rose: hey doun doun derrie doun

                hey doun doun
                doun derrie doun

**two years next month / since my last poetry volume**

two years next month
since my last poetry volume
two years without a single line   dark

without even a thought that could go towards a poem

this is how I want my life   this
writingless styptic
of this house: every child

ironed   folded neatly   handed over warm as the word home

this is what I say and this is how I pencil
ruins around me   cold and
misplaced?   bending away each

housemate searches for silence  breath  light – a safe cone

stop all correspondence   translation
rhyming analysis and come sit
in front of this clean page

how does one begin a poem?

sharp Turkish-red pencil   fragrant rubber
I cleave my ears inwards
tap at the inner walls trying to intercept the tremors

*what* is it that I want to say   my inside remains mute as stone

desperately I begin to flog every scar
let marrow dance against the scabs
my palm on the woven page bloodily sweats its knowledge:

each lived, each poemed is granted only through that inner groan

## once more / before an empty page

*once more*
*before an empty page    unlined    A4*

softly an opening begins to pout
something quivers through    my breathing lessens

to a restrained graze    I wait
pencil point just above the page

already I detect the slight fibre-pulsing
my senses lightly bump against each other

*far off a child calls / a door slams / footsteps come down the passage*

I grab at the opening – even a spattering will do!
urgently caress the already closing muscle

a deadness shoots up from my feet    I stand in front of a smooth wall

*a child enters the room warily / are you busy? / his eyes grey and shredded*

**Kroonstad**
**March '86**

Dear S.
yes, I am the she who chords tresses of verse
      and the wind thereof is my body;
who yearns for our unheard-of sort
      we who beggarly curse the terse page;
who navigate midlight and untiringly spin
      wordpurses from the pencil's spindle;
I am on the lookout for a woman with language and transparent seas
      who can dry-dock on paper;
I don't think forth in poems
      but in volumes and the pure ice of it;
when my body's like this I plunge overboard
      if I don't immerse her in the biographical Word.

A.

P.S. I found several names: Augusta de Mist, Mrs Koopmans de Wet & Lady Anne Lindsay (Barnard). Will look into them.

## hail Lady Anne Barnard!

Hail Lady Anne Barnard!
Your life I wish to celebrate, prising
Chords from it for our African part.
I curtsey, bow and kiss your hand:
Be my guide, I – your anxious bard!

# Cape of Good Hope
# 4th May – 1797

## Journal

First the gannets nostril-less with ink-lined eyes,
later shrill branch-clawed seagulls, then a dark fringe
of hollow seaweed bringing a soft drift of mistlike
vines. The land shrouds itself in secrecy.

A light breeze shifts us into the harbour
and then, for our deck-perplexed group
an embossed pageant: as if
by invisible nod, the fog lifts

and Lion's Rump flicks the vapour from her croup;
without guile Lion's Head lets fall
the necklace of vapours circling her stupendous throat –
*up* over the naked swollen stone feet, slyly, draws

the stage curtain and *there* is the mountain – all
perpendicular rock, sullen and winecoloured. Massive.
Its dourness hidden under the white damask tablecloth
hanging halfway down its side, dwarfing

the toy block houses and buildings
that step neatly out of the bay.
With gun and cannon salvos our arrival
is acknowledged. In the first boat sway

Macartney and Barnard and now that I approach
the white beach punctuated by soldiers,
I suddenly feel, alas, how my intended
best, so conscientiously spelled out to Dundas,

is being overwhelmed by a flaunting haughtiness.
Coolly I set my buttoned-up shoe on the beach
and wave the carriage sent for me away. My simple smock
of lawn-silk and muslin sneers my class to the bay.

*

Barnard's gone to bed long since
in the bedstead with silk taffeta fringes of *chocolate* brown
– the furuncle on his lip
pulses under an alum potion.

In the cabin, with Macartney
and Sir James Craig – I saw him
everywhere with his eyes slightly bulging
with nerves, tenderly stroking the swelling

And I want to lead him out, my young one,
so that we stretch out our hands together
to this dry darkness and feel: cool its stone,
mild its earth, both smelling the wildness

of narcissus, humanless and pale, I want to hold him
linked to all of this first night.
Suddenly he groans, rips off the sheets, his bonewhite
ankle stained with bites! I salute you, Africa, in ink!

# Part II

**Cape of Good Hope**
10th July – 1797

**To Henry Dundas**

Nothing less than a princess! I've inherited a hall of 60 ft
a drawing room of 40, 3 supper rooms and on the upper
floor endless bedrooms. Green ceilings that I now
have painted white. Black floors bowing
with finesse in cadmium yellow; wallpaper removed (together
with mice and rats); the whitewashed walls receive an eye-level

pale purple border. First Thursday of every month I have
Publick Day: (found a dozen black fiddlers to play!)
full-chested women in dresses from different pasts
furtively dance a kind of pit-a-pat step: their husbands
to the side sway in pipe smoke and jokes.
The castle, gland of light purified

by sheep's tail fat, hangs in haze and flame
over my guests' grotesque teeth, their swollen throats,
beam-broad hands delicately taking aim
at oyster pies and mushroom tarts. Lord Macartney
provides our parties with exotic tales and names
from Russia, Caribbean and one night talked

of a ball in Batavia where at midnight
everybody changed into bedclothes – the ladies in light
skin-thin gowns of gold cloth, hair plaited as if for sleep,
barefoot, naked arms with an unexpected exposure
of pulse veins. In a whirl of wine and food
the last dance is danced in an unswerving exhilarated mood.

**Castle
October 1797**

**villanelle for a refreshment station**

they cling transparent ochre to stone and rusted ironwrought
leaves of Capse Rose and Rosa odorata flourish in the fountain
from the Peacock Room a strange light devours the inner court

since our arrival this spot has shuddered in my brain
out of autumn gossamer the sun produced a splendid snare
leaves of Capse Rose and Rosa odorata flourish in the fountain

in each sketch the light rambles towards you but nought
captures your cape the allure of your neck slightly turned
from the Peacock Room a strange light devours the inner court

brittle alabaster your axils where sprigs sprout in textures of tin
threads of woven southern light have taken us in tow
leaves of Capse Rose and Rosa odorata flourish in the fountain

oh it's only paradise I sought where the sun lords
and drifts towards us in fluent glories of sea and mountain blue
from the Peacock Room a strange light devours the inner court

beloved    I have uncovered a continent for us thus bought
by famous apostles to contain all our hesitant ecstasies
leaves of Capse Rose and Rosa odorata flourish in the fountain
from the Peacock Room a strange light devours the inner court

## Castle
## 12th Oct. – 1797

## Journal

Through a fanlight tinting the small tiles I
have liveried my ardent husband years younger
than me at his side. Blind I can draw
the power of his jawline. His jaunty eyes lounge
past me. We dance, he leads, my hand lightly in his.
From this side I can sketch his short thumb
(ink on the middle finger)."Nanny dearest!"
his mouth too tender for pen or martenhair brush.

The woman with the yellow eyes, pickled teeth
in her roguish mouth, brings her vain lips to his ear –
quickly I draw him winking, fill in the curls over his pleated collar,
the beginning of beard specks. She wants to bed him,
I fear… The shiny bust in chintz wants to bed
my husband. I turn my back so as to refrain
from signalling: to unseat me does not sit
in your paltry baleen, my ill-bred dutchfaced dear

(my mockery later about the little plebeian will quickly
knife the whole flirtation – I will not so easily allow
this country to defile my life).

**Castle
1798**

**Journal**

it is midnight and pewter
outside    from the balcony
the stained gardens breathe
around me    I hear the garrison
and lust after you
already two weeks since you left
at the Imari basin
I imagine you shaving
from behind I burrow into softer

flesh    how robust the seam how virulently
your shirt swells out glides down
ashamed am I of my desire: to grab you by the hips
from behind    grow male
not to ride a broomstick but
to bloody fuck you between tincool buttocks into a presence

# Auld Robin Gray
## written by Lady Anne Barnard

When the sheep are in the fauld, and the kye's come hame,
And a' the weary warld to rest are gane,
The waes o' my heart fa' in showers frae my e'e,
Unkent by my gudeman, wha sleeps sound by me.

Young Jamie lo'ed me weel, and sought me for his bride;
But saving ae crown-piece he had naething else beside:
To make the crown a pound, young Jamie gaed to sea;
And the crown and the pound – they were baith for me.

He hadna been gane awa' a twelvemonth and a day,
When my father brake his arm, and the cow was stown away;
My mither she fell sick, – and my Jamie was at sea,
And Auld Robin Gray came a courting me.

My father couldna wark – and my mither couldna spin –
I toiled day and night, but their bread I couldna win, –
Auld Rob maintained them baith, and, wi' tears in his e'e
Said, "Jeanie, O for their sakes will ye no marry me?"

My heart it said na; and I looked for Jamie back;
But hard blew the winds, and his ship was a wrack;
His ship was a wrack – why didna Jamie dee?
Or why am I spared to cry wae is me?

My father urged me sair: my mither didna speak,
But she looked in my face till my heart was like to break;
They gied him my hand – my heart was in the sea –
And so Robin Gray he was gudeman to me.

I hadna been a wife a week but only four,
When, mournfu' as I sat on the stane at the door,
I saw my Jamie's ghaist, for I couldna think it he,
Till he said, 'I'm come hame, love, to marry thee!'

O sair, sair did we greet, and mickle say of a',
I gied him ae kiss, and bade him gang awa', –
I wish that I were dead, but I'm na like to dee;
For though my heart is broken, I'm but young, wae is me!

I gang like a ghaist, and I carena much to spin,
I darena think o' Jamie, for that wad be a sin;
But I'll do my best a gude wife to be,
For, O, Robin Gray, he is kind to me.

## Gossip from diaries and letters

"Lady Anne moved in here on Berkeley Square –
so thick with the royals her Scottish accent's disappeared."

"From her windows she can just see without light
William Windham arriving home at night."

"Aye! To survive royalty requires more than Highland breeding –
your legs must be strong my friend, ready for a balling."

\*

"Lady Garrick says that Lady Anne's morning frock
has a visible tear. If she mends it she acknowledges poverty.
So at every tea party with bystanders she is newly shocked!"

"Good heavens, how old is he?" "Fifteen years
younger they say – not royalty – and penniless; at the age
of thirty already booked off the military for ill health fears."

"Yes who knows? The wedding ring of a wife raised
many a nobody to the higher terraces of social life."

## Old Lady Lindsay from Scotland

The character of Mr Barnard
is a treasure that will last
both in this world and that
which is to come, but one
fault, viz., being too young,

but one cannot have everything.

## To Windham
## 1st Nov. – 1793

nothing I do interests you any more    this
I know    but your indifference has always been
preferable to your absence    however this
I have to tell you in person – my hand keenly
reaching out to your skin – oh, it will be missed

yesterday I married Andrew Barnard in St George's
in Hanover Square    I know the news
does not even smell of malice

but my harbour is now insured against sorrow
I burrow where no capricious loving
or coldness or whim
or passion or infidelity
can humiliate or dim or ravish me
any more (or ever again)

**St Wolstans near Dublin**
**10th Dec. – 1793**

**To Henry Dundas**

Poverty forces us to rent out everything.
For the sake of our friendship, please endure

my pleas; you do owe me a little
happiness, truly, it is so. Don't you

want to make good by giving a post
to the man who is rebuilding my life

and restoring my youth, where both of us
can work for our benefit but mostly for yours?

Dublin
12th July – 1794

## To Henry Dundas

After my confidential visit
I was bothered by the many motives
that are among our crippling
feelings for each other.

You are just –
above all generous
you distribute posts like presents
to family members.

You owe me Dundasdear
and this pleading to you
beats against my partner's
plebeian ear.

**Kroonstad
first state of emergency
July 1985**

by early sunrise the sleeping town is already
surrounded by convoys forking on flyovers,
filtering further    at night back from
visiting friends in the district a sleeping hive
of children held close – road blockades, flashing lights
a cold gun barrel somewhere behind    staring at a nest
of flycatchers birds and antelope suddenly
in flight from veld shadows – low over buckshot
three impala planes fly to the north
news reports: family eliminated. so, a child stops a tea-time bullet
with his tongue but television and newspapers mark the March
of the Morons and talk endlessly about HIV

rhyme-footed I crawl through the dark forbidden lines
to lay my ear irrevocably against the poetic divine

**first Christmas weekend
under the second state of emergency
1988**

we murmur on the verandah at dusk
it's as if ears stir in the ivy
strung in blood around the house and fences
unexpected forms wait in the shade
we hesitate
opened letters fall into the house
someone runs up the street
we wait
the garden rustles in mists of suspicion
we speak more softly
so many children in prison
so many arrests
the trains moan restlessly
is it true
so many thousands of children?
rumours crawl from the foundations like rats

christmas cookies ginger beer a little tree
children play with cousins
the turkey hisses stuffed with tarragon thyme and raisins
under bows of light families bob in boats
the river slushes against the keels
crackers crack
black workers at the mooring place look up
unfathomably

I play the piano my children dressed
as Mary and Joseph and angel sing:
   *away in a manger*
   *a trough for his bed*

*(translated by Karen Press)*

**because among mine I feel more and more ill at ease**

because among mine I feel more and more ill at ease
feel my church sitting ever broader and unchurchlike
glittering    and black is indeed a colour passionately bleeding us into one
oh I sing from a book in a language
that is not mine in tongues that I do not know
the tenor clear in front I let myself be led
the sopranos embrace the altos fill
bass voices carry God, does He hear us? whence the urge
to restore?    that we all just want to human    I with less
they with more and I hear the swelling of a mighty
grief. force circumscribing my white retort

**to have or to be**

1.
- be in possession of
- keep available
- more or less always accessible
- be part of
- enjoy the advantages of
- contain
- carry within you
- keep at your disposal
- gather interest

the habit of having and holding on

it never changes its appearance
though it looks like us
even the moment
it is used as auxiliary verb

2.
the child whose
parents have both died
can exist
as copulative verb
actualised

**gnome**

after the umpteenth family row over politics
(this poem could also be titled the umpteenth political row in the family)
despite the admonition
of the head of the family:
stick to small talk
even the word microwave
has loaded meaning
the question who drinks their coffee white
a final choice
old grievances get a political gloss
while faces minted from the same coin
shout at each other
fists thunder on tables
softer voices plead with hand gestures for a turn to speak
it is definitely clear
our language's glossary
lies chiefly in the genitive

## parole

I feel I lie because I blatantly indulge
in words
and useless eras
in the face of so much injustice
if poetry perseveres as luxury it also becomes a lie

I live on the other side of injustice
therefore I have the time
to tune chords precisely around the private gland
and why not? this country
has already been ruined

the order comes: words should be AK47s
should always fight    poetry should be useable
deed    relate the struggle    take sides
weeds are mightier than roses
tortured poetry grows wild in phonetic rain

(how can I safeguard
this poem against the stupidity
of politics? distressed
I stand, looked upon with suspicion,
my most ordinary words refused)

I am shamed by the poet's unheard of poetry
which screams on the other side of all breath
there where your eyes stop now: gravel road
spaza someone may have disappeared
before dawn; the wind moves as if in war
children kick a ball in the townships where three quarters

of the world lives and waits rightly so
for equality    shy like you    brave
or stupid or perhaps already lazy and corrupt like
us    from their hands hangs this treacherous carpet
of hope and hunger and dream

but the poet stands aside
he hears of petitions
motions of injustice
he has stopped writing poems
no poetry
the thoughtful poet stands smokeblue with cold

barely audible
she repeats her arrest
her sentence
melts from her tongue
not in print
not in photographs
not in statistics
everywhere it is damp
rumours of disappearances
torture
and anonymous deaths

the struggle filters
through with inaudible fierce noises
into the shady
suburbs
this has become a country of rumours

if my senses
cannot wean the cries from the leaves
or the blood from the barricades of groceries
or pick up murder from the blockades near my desk
I will die hardened
in the crossfire of pencil and paper
which always fight back to the truth
all the writers are dead aren't they
they can't write "about" or "of" the oppressed
and the oppressed writer is drowning in anger
– this is what's being said
"aesthetics is the only ethic"
they say as well
but the demands do not tolerate neutral ground

between two evils I choose neither

I was born
of a guild
of greed and scorn
where I always felt myself apart

a hedge between myself
and them   myself and the slaughter

nothing ever prepared me for hunger and homelessness
landlessness   I try to find a bridge
but everything is burning and I am looking for a guide

beware of propaganda   rhetoric
coarse chains of words under the whip of lies
without even the charm of consciousness
is aesthetics ever useful?

I never stop
studying
survival
with this fragile most light-hearted category
I diligently investigate every relation
to breathe to breathe yes to breathe
language has never been useless or fake

but only   although the poet may desire indulgence
and the progression of political words
the injustice is real
and whatever I write which will survive
sprouts from the feudal clash between lyddite and lie

*(after reading Carolyn Forché and Stephen Watson)*

## cape of good hope

computerised city –
programmed underground
fine figured
power goes its terrible way

from your cybernetic memory
I want to take back my life
and my honour
and my name
all of it destroyed by the times we live in     hear me

out:     I refuse to witness any longer
        I refuse your decoding of freedom
        I want to take my life back from you

also:    who does this word serve?
        how do I understand myself in this text-tortured land
        how untouched do I hover?

freedom has already been
won in word and grenade
it has been taken     I
hear the sound of a thousand footfalls
oh do not pass me by

## Lady Anne as guide because a hero needs a bard

I wanted to live a second life through you
Lady Anne Barnard – show it is possible
to hone truth with the pen
to live an honourable life within so much privilege

weave a language of revolution and conspiracies
liberate slaves   clinically plunder royalty
and with your expedition through the interior
cleave the boers to the bone

but from your letters you emerge
hand on the hip talented
but a frivolous fool, pen
in crafty ink, snob, naive liberal

being swayed away from your principles
by your useless husband's pampering
you never had real pluck
now that your whole puerile life

has arrived on my desk, I go berserk: as metaphor
my Lady, you're not worth a fuck

## "I think I am the first" – Lady Anne on Table Mountain

you cannot paint it   colour will clench
the walking into waterfall gossamer
from ravine and stone   around us
the mountain paws the ground sifting softly
in the mist   everything held safely by name
go
please go why wait   so tiny suddenly our struggling
figures in the gritty trench

of words but your feet beloved mountaineer assembled
in tomato-red socks and climbing boots
move peacefully from stone to stone
to my myopic eyes the mist becomes lace
when our two figures are pegged against the rock face
where only damp sweeps between cheek and stone –
stained with roots of heather and proteas
hanging like rucksacks of birds – zip-like colours scrambling


the climb wipes out everything settled
between us we become part of the slippery tongue-talking
mountain my blood pulses thinner than thin
as we go higher and higher, see
your secure footstep always in front of me
skull-wet rain along our hot throat-skins
from Platteklip Gorge the wind boring
down on everything which is small and settler

naked the abyss – the route more dense
forcing us closer   how do I preserve this memory
my fellow poet of beauty because everything is
destructible   except the tongue against
which we stretch so small   the soft shower of the sea sketches

itself far below you turn the colour of your eyes smudged
and lonely in your mouth lies the unbearable intimacy of consonance

from above you can really sketch everything
corruption seems only malicious
injustice temporary
and at its worst
the *dorpje* below dares
to be nothing but shoddy
see how delicious the stonypoint castle   (my pretty abode!)
oh my God do we have to? we sing: save George our King

the wet clothes in front of the fire though trite
compel us to break through layers of isolation
how do I bring this rainblind excursion into words?
new words for survival
without destroying the vital
breathless preciousness of sheltering each other
both knowing
how mercilessly it destroys *between* the times we write

# Part III (V)

# The Drup Kelder
# Tuesday 8th May – 1798

## Journal

A day of miracle and wonder against the white
dune mountains where hunters like tiny wishbones
spin after hare and antelope. Along a ledge of rock edges
we move step by step, bright petticoats of foam spatter
the corners of our eyes –
at last we shuffle into the cellars'
dome. Last lit for high society in Berkeley Square my candles find
to their shock, their "tails" now shimmering African caves alight.

The men turn back. I sit alone in the silent sweaty heart –
drops peaking and falling into what looks like sandy blood
deeper in misshapen limbs wrestle, ribs distend from crushed
figures   furious howls petrify into barbaric gut.
Fattened nails claw against stone. I see iron bars slam
against bloodied bone, while it could all be pearly –
Aladdin or blissful glut – if only I had the courage to turn;
but like a smoking pit, sick of the vision, into the cold sea air I gasp

# Farm of Jakob van Reenen
# Sunday 13th May – 1798

## Journal

In the lamplight wait bunches of children, blond of every hue;
a slave beside each one. To pots of tea and coffee on the coals
the hostess points "mak-self-knowsbest-vat-like." Dinner:
juicy roast veal and in its rich gravy swirls an oryx stew

a curry soup with rice, partridges spliced
and done on the gridiron; for dessert there is biltong
butter and very tolerable apples. We are shown
a stinkwood bed with clean heavy bedding

and sleep "like the sons of Kings" – perhaps better.

## Monday 14th May – 1798

### Journal

Early this morning we rocked in a wagon
over the grassy plains where game stream
until all horizons collapse; partridges like
whirring buttons and from the grass nineteen ostriches

bolted clear – their eyes riveted like washers to sticks.
Bontebok, steinbok spindly as devil's thorn; springbok flick
tiny white fans in their frisky jolting arches from the herd-splash;
plump zebra tails broad as barbels hang from glazed lilac backs

(my drawing book stoutly on my knee); I see the soapy
entrances wedged between their striped hind legs.
Among the noise and gunpowder my husband's eyes
jeer with a kind of ownership I both desire and fear.

## Tuesday 15th May – 1798

## Journal

Sails are thrown open on flat slabs of reef.
I sketch the river – a boat arrives loaded
with claws of fish. Gaspar makes a fire.
Mrs van Reenen issues orders and rolls up her sleeves.

With my sketch the meal is ready and we
sit down under the silvery mane of willows:
salt, pepper, mustard in tiny calabashes; pitchforks
arrive with spitted fish roasted on an open flame;

a pan of butter, lemon, soya and cayenne
fish soup with rice, a hotchpotch of smaller river fish.
The nets are being hauled again:
a skate as big as a house: it sighs bitterly

and dies with difficulty. Eels with bills like woodcocks
are cut up by the hostess, hung and then pickled
in Martaban jars. Lying back, drowsy with sweet wine
and sun Mr van Reenen begins to tell of places –

ferns frocked with the lightest green; a desert delta
where hippos gallop along the bottom;
minarets above thorn trees; a white woman
of the Abelungu tribe combing her long hair all day long.

"Why do you live here then?" Van Reenen hestitates:
"As one journeys, the coastline in one's head grows longer,
one's island-heart smaller and stripped of inanities.
Every journey makes you read your life with a new monocle

and the Cape is such a disgusting little whine. Authentic this
authentic that and fully immoral. Besides neither myself
nor my neighbours like to work – here we breed horses,
hunt, everybody has enough and peace is not clandestine.

Or what do you say, my wife?" He takes her hand
and looks down at her – her face rosy and kind,
her soft body swollen around their umpteenth
child and I read a rapport between them which

presses home my bland barren body and smarting
marriage. Before we leave I hand out small
scissors, cloth, thread, strings of white beads
for the girls. Late at night there is a soft call

from my door: slave Dunira pleads for some
of the beads. But how can I give the same
to master and slave? I gesture that there are
no more left. Next morning van Reenen laughs

at me – this frame of mind is quite unnecessary –
Dunira is a freeborn and besides everybody
in this house knows: the more you have
the more you owe.

## Tuesday 22nd May – 1798

## Journal

One solitary farmhouse is superimposed
on the next. So too the morbid figures
eating: breakfast, oleaginous lunch,
light nap, fie! then cake with coffee, fatty dinner

surrounded by formless women, children shouting
at slaves, vapours of rat, smelly meat, fleas, dirty sheets,
randy daughters watching Mr Barnard's neat
morning ablutions as they polish glasses with a nightcap.

At Gelukwaard this couple: she married
for love, he the old woman for money.
"We farmed, progressed, bought neighbouring
farms, did transport and running

exclusive markets for fleet owners.
Then one night, he abandoned me."
Her fingers thread the fringes
of her shawl: "Believe you me

when a woman is at her smartest,
her strongest, her most principled –
then the pathetic miscreant behind her leaves!
Astutely he calculated his cards: from then on

she spends the rest of her life
gathering the shards."

## St Andrew's Fife
## Scotland 25th Aug. – 1987

In the hotel's attic we lie on our beds and look out over the wet slate roofs. Eat our last cheeses, olives, smoked meat, drink wine from hotel glasses, while Dean Martin sings: memories are made of this.

We go for a walk. Far. In the ruin of St Andrew's Castle I look through a dressed stone window frame out over the grey sea. Exactly so it would have looked centuries ago to somebody looking through this very window. Other clothes she would have worn, other sounds in the background, other foods in her stomach juices, other agonies in her thoughts, other interpreters on her tongue, but what she saw, what she was looking through, then, was the same as now, here, for me. At half-past nine that evening the Earl phones. I break into a sweat over the telephone receiver. My English breaks into a few barbaric phrases.

## visit to Balcarres

Colinsburgh is a small village on the A921 at the gates of the Balcarres Estate – built in the nineteenth century for returning soldiers. Side gate. Narrow stone passage with relics. Up the steps. Double doors opening. A man stretching out his arms: Ah my guests from Africa! And when he finally stands in front of me, this descendant of a woman who has been my obsession for so many years, I have to make a complete change of course: I have underestimated her class. Because I suddenly wrestle with a knee that wants to curtsey, a hand that wants to salute, an intimidation to pay tribute. Lord Robert Lindsay is the 29th Earl of Crawford and Balcarres; has clear light-blue eyes, silver-grey hair and a face that can only be described as brittle refinement. (Educated I am in their alphabet of symbols.)

Portraits of family members and friends painted by Romney and Gainsborough hang everywhere. Lady Anne's bedroom window looks out on the Firth of Forth with Edinburgh hazily on the far horizon. Enamel bowls on the steps: Mind the leaks, the Earl says, civilised. Enormous battered Persian carpets, wallpaper from the east older than two hundred years. "But here is what you came to see..." He takes out books half a metre in size from the bookshelves. Carefully he extracts one from its leatherbound holder: on the left are the letters and recollections, on the right the drawings and watercolours. The composed greens and greys gradually make way for colour and light: that breaks behind mountains, that cuts the wall like a thin sword; silver trees in wild chignons of silvergreen, bunches of stiff proteas, scenes where the overwhelming light leaves all colours colourless.

Even the pen-and-ink sketches are afflicted by light. There is something soft, somewhat whimsically too easy in her figures of darker colour; something curt in the boers, and always in profile. A precision she bestows on the architecture with a wildness in the landscape beside it. The colours, after nearly two hundred years, glow cordially from these sketches in the dismal Scottish light. "She insisted on the best paper and inks, always." The original journal of her journey to the interior is opened carefully. I am too scared to page. The Earl shows me an inscription on the cover page: "Every page is a page of struggle. I write to destroy the borders of pain." The Earl and I look each other in the eye.

After the visit, my husband and I drink a beer in the tedious American bar of the Balcarres Hotel in Colinsburgh. We put a pound in the whiskey bottle with the notice: guide dogs for the blind.

## the ballad of Andries Dundas-Dekker

in my confirmation suit
I joined a ship
celebrated my freedom
with coke 'n rum whips

one night smoking
too much fennel
I passed out
among the lower deck kennels

when logs of light
pounded my eyes
a girl descended from a dizzy
height: "and where's my dog?"

for long afterwards we
corresponded    I read
between the lines: she
wanted to wed my body

"you want to marry?" I
tempted fate. "yes,
but here on Arniston Estate"
are you crazy?

"we marry at Groblersdal
where I was born"
in Windhoek we married
without family or qualm

and after the honeymoon
elated we drove
an old car down the
Arniston road stopped

in front of, my eyes popped, a
fucking mansion with staff lined up
at the door: ah miss Agatha miss
Agatha they chimed I threw my suitcase

back in the boot "let me go home"
"Darling, wait, let's put
shoulder to the wheel
remember: through thick and thin"

what she was hinting was: this place
was short of boere piel because everything
was falling apart and drenched in winter rot
that first winter we all nearly died

"send me 50 kaffirs, the whole
lot in May," I pleaded
just to get this place fixed
we worked night and day

chased animals into the gardens
turned l'Orangerie into
a forgery   forbade entry
all descendants had to pay

to see their dynasty
millionaires we were
but beggars –
oh how to have and be free

*That night we sleep peacefully in the nursery of the Dundas's Adam mansion – in a long room on a copper double bed, down duvet and hand-embroidered appliqué sheets. Suddenly I am awake deep in the night and hear how quiet it is. As if I find myself in the heartest heart of silence.*

*Then next morning we look out at the endless landscape of misty green trees and hear the sound of hundreds of birds. In the simple guest apartment where they live we take leave. And they remain standing, half close to each other, half separate in front of their majestic house while we travel down the small road into our own ordinary lives.*

**Genadendal
10th May – 1798**

**Journal**

Three Moravian brothers give us lodging
without ostentation. Late afternoon the bell
(heard even in Stellenbosch) tolls
through the valley. Prayer meeting.
We sit with timidity
face to a hundred and fifty faces.

My coat, I remember suddenly, is wrinkled; they clothed somewhat
in skin. The clay floor under reed mats cut
by languid sunlight. My coat remains
with me. I smell them, they me. The missionary
lifts his hands and says simply: *myne lieve vriende...*

and suddenly in this simplicity I perceive Him –
quiet like a clear bubble in my brain. Before Him
we are all naked, but I see, as always, He sides with them:
the hungry, the poor, the crowds without hope
the silent stubble, those without rights.
He becomes human in this rough building and turns to look at me:

it is good to be here, it is good.
I remember my own church – the velvet matrix
filled with stones and corrupt chattering and I feel
God, how far away from You am I? How narrowly I know
still only myself – tired of white coinage
and they? The combers of wigs,

the polishers of silver, the whitewashers of walls –
they know apart from themselves also my innermost bed.
What is it that I must *do*? How do I get rid
of this white exclusive stain? Unexpectedly a song
swells into garish passionate grief
all-powerful in pain. (For the past or what is still to come?)

I sit surrendered in liturgical darkness:
my wrists frayed, my lips dense with blood
my head hangs in the softest sweat.
Before the closing prayer the missionary folds his hands
relentlessly to my side into the eye of a needle.

*

I cut the ham into thin fragrant petal bundles
at which the Herrnhuters greedily stab with their forks
swiping through mustard: *"Broeder,* eat this!"
Our casks of Madeira and gin splash festively
into cups. I don't hear it. I don't see it.
Outside the moon grates herself insanely on the mountains.

More than millions tonight are huddling close to fires, rough
bread and beer, songs, stories drifting from the coals...
How do I give up this snug cavity into which I was born?
Turn! Distribute! And my overstuffed soul? Isn't it simply looking
for something new to thrill at? Shouldn't every settler
carry her bundle of gold and rot in respectable regret?

(Even the choice stinks of privilege.)
While the night still lies in the valley
blood bursts on the peaks. I get up: sable brushes, inks,
water. I drink some coffee, bread, cold meat.
My fingers clumsy with my coat. Along the footpath
my eyes scout for heights. Quickly stretch pages, mix greens, yes

green is the colour of balance, green endures
beyond all colours, green is constantly broken
to absorb closer and further,
black is only a shade of the deepest green,
in watercolour white is forbidden; dimension
comes from exclusion....

I have to find a framework for the complete landscape
if I want to survive: pitching the valley into perspective,
the rest will follow, but something moves between me and the sun.
The Gaspar holds the umbrella. I wave him impatiently
out of the way, but it's too late – the fixed sun bursts
brutally from above and drums the mission station into a colourless mirage.

I get nothing on paper. Nothing fits, the scale is wrong. I aim. I start
afresh. I stare until it dawns on me: my pages for ever
spell "window," spell distance, the angle of entering always passive.
So this is the way Madame wants to live here: observing the country
safely through glass – wrapping it in pretty pictures and rhymes.
But. I could slowly pull back my hand and pick up a stone,

I could throw it, shatter the glass to gulp    to thaw retchingly
in this hip-high landscape swirling with wild abundance and abuse.

# Thursday 31st May – 1798

## Journal

Lunch on Blaauwberg Pass. Gaspar races
through the dark, rushing full speed along the beach
while the tide foams in under our wheels.
The horses muffled and fearful – fleeing from quicksand
or thick spots of loam. We hear the thumping behind us.
At eight o'clock we clatter with a drone of southeaster
and rain in frantic haste through the lit Castle gateway
that I, inexplicably, experience as home.

# Wyk 5

# Wyk 5

## Stem vir

Ek beloof om my hiervoor te beywer:
1. Herinstelling van aandklokreël vir anderskleuriges in blanke gebiede (21h00 tot 05h00).
2. Swart huurmotorstaanplek sal verskuif word na die openbare park op die hoek van Piet de Vrieslaan en Stasiestraat.
3. Kroonpark slegs vir blankes.
4. Speelparke in woonbuurte slegs vir blankes.

**Dink hieroor na en stem dan reg op 26 Oktober 1988**

Opgestel en uitgegee deur  Kroonstad en gedruk deur Kroonstad  Drukkers, Murraystraat

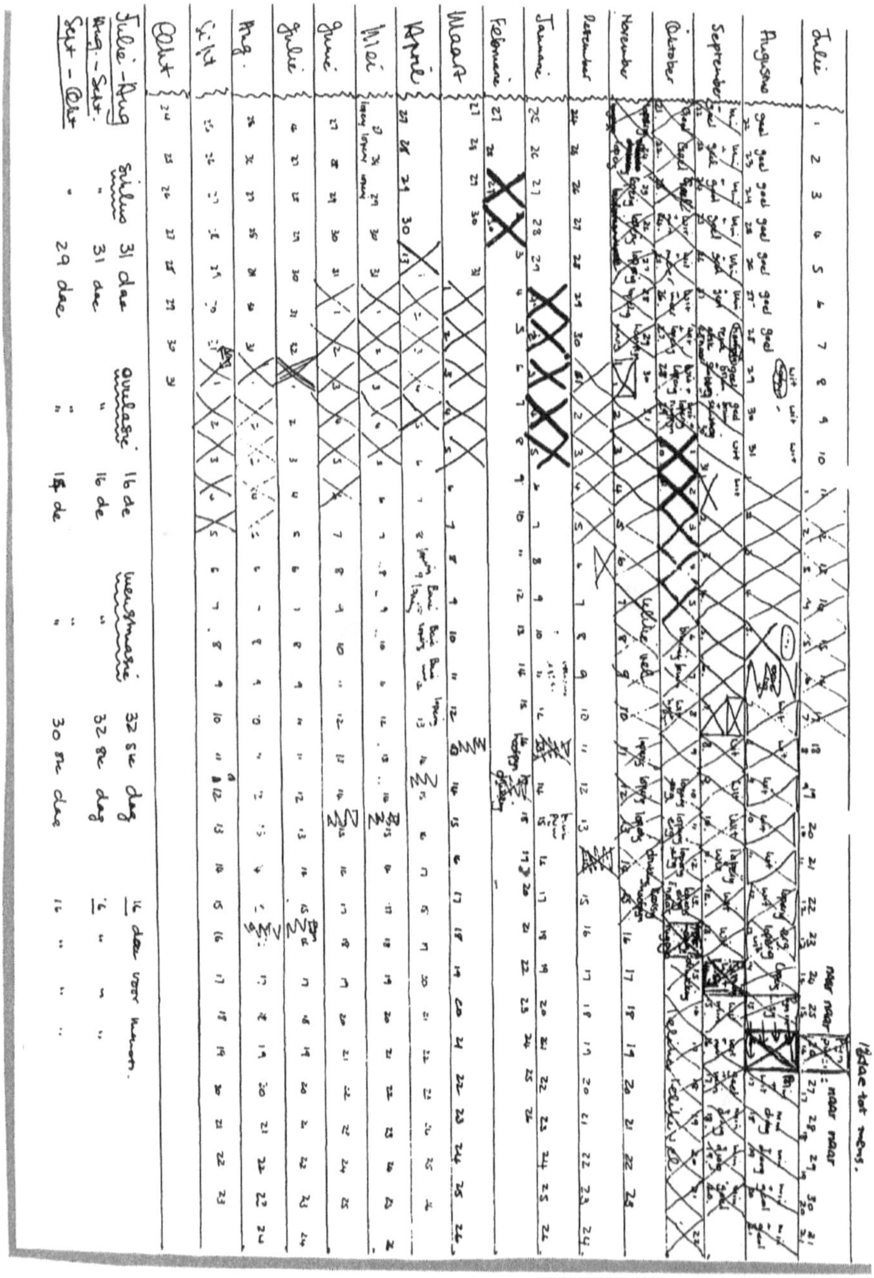

# Part IV

"A great writer," Brodsky maintains, "is one who elongates the perspective of human sensibility, who shows a man at the end of his wits an opening a pattern to follow."

Lettie Viljoen het vrae gestel om te probeer vasstel waarvoor die gehoor gekom het: wat verwag hulle om te hoor? Dat skrywers anders is as ander teksproduseerders? Dat hulle 'n diagnose kan gee van 'n siekte? Vooraan die "struggle" moet wees? Moet hulle soos God sien, met 'n omvattende oog van Bloukrans tot by Crossroads?

It is demonstrably true that at no other time in history have writers respondend so intensely to the problems of men and women in society as they have in this century. (...) With his or her eyes no longer turned to God, with any answer to human needs less and less often conceived in metaphysical terms, the writer's focus on the earth and consequent awareness of the material causes for so many matters formerly held to be immutable, has grown insistent and brought with it an increased sense of responsibility. For the twentieth-century writer not only has politics in all its forms – as theory, as commitment, as action – become a matter of consciousness, of conscience, often involving the subordination of aesthetic considerations to socio-political demands, but secularization itself has entailed the belief, now widespread, that the true creator, the really responsible writer, is the one who makes others *act*.

"Art is not a better, but an alternative existence; it is not an attempt to escape reality but the opposite, an attempt to animate it."

'Because, as I suggested earlier, in South Africa the colonisation of the novel by the discourse of history is proceeding with alarming rapidity.'

(...) it is precisely the function of this form of ideological thinking to produce a parody, a caricatured version of that which is, in reality, invariably that much more diverse and complex. It creates that alternately arid and terrifying mindlessness of which Kundera speaks, that seemingly insurmountable Manicheism which will, it sometimes seems, last long after the demise of the present cartel of murderers and thieves that rules this country.

"Die vraag is," sê Hein Willemse:
"Waar was die Afrikaanse skrywers toe die land gebrand het?"

20th Nov. – 1798

## Journal

Macartney drove out to the Roundhouse for the last time.
Among flower rampages in fragrant pipettes of colour
he picked shoots of Love-lies-bleeding
and saluted the lime
cliffs at Schoenmaker's Gat leaning
into a crude hairdo of birds. See how withered
his wave is – all shrivelled up. Turning back to the chaste
mountainlip something somehow loomed in its curves.
The cottage at Paradise couldn't exorcise our sense of doom
– nor the avenues of oak or pines
nor the orchards polishing orange medallion groves
nor the wolf with its womb nor the cobra with its muscular gown.
Windeberg's cap tilted more and more askew. For you
I am glossing my inadaptability from afar in fallow blue strophes.

**Paradise
November 1798**

**To Henry Dundas**

This letter was supposed to have left with Lord Macartney –
our rheumatic amulet against this place.
Last night a fire broke out
in the sheds
with flame-crowns hosed
by a southeaster
yawing all we have gathered in barns. In the

dragoon stables the white porcelain eyes of horses already long-legged
in flames – 130 burnt to death
a thundering breach of oats, barley
among bricks a
light purple flame-nest
funnelling through
barrels of rose oil, brandy, vinegar – bubbling Nanking urns swallowing

flame and sighingly slaked with delicate twigs. The calamity
was confirmed: en route to the ship
we saw the whole beach covered
in an unheard of convulsion
of ocean: a
fresh grizzly brocade –
fish drifting on rafts of froth and polyps   Pawell held out

to us naked slugs with mantles, eggs rolled in
a husky yellow rose   snakes with swimming
tails, thick-faced fish, evil curdled
eyes already
excavated by
lines of beach fleas, sea lice with their greedy grapeshot

# 1789

## Windham's Paris

One brusque winter he showed me
wordless episodes:

- A lady kneeling
  in her coach to fit
  her roof-high hair

- An eclipse around
  the dazzling skin
  of Marie Antoinette

- Fan-codes the only language:
  2 taps: I languish
  a light tap on the cuff: we are being watched

I could feel
Windham wanting to lay down
something in me
he had an urgency
an impatience with my fondling eyes
that could not believe
that for so many hours he was moving
within my frame his face
sweaty his skin thinly splinted
around his frost-bound passion of ice

- Hour after hour
  the coach windows
  show me in mezzo tint:

  Neighbourhood after neighbourhood
  slums, shacks, furrows of distress
  ploughed up from the snow

- "The firewood lies ready for a revolution
  Anne, which will not simply change
  the rider on the horse

  But a revolution that will renew
  everything: will bring a new awareness
  between man and his fellow man"

Tears stream down my neck
I grind his agile fingers
between my hands
unbearable the weight of my hopeless
love my desperate yearning
for his head against my breast
the language of his tempestuous dreams
without which I cannot live:

- You are the first man
  whose equal
  I *want* to be

# 1793

When Dundas with his thick accent
asked me formally for my hand, he dealt
me a trump to force Windham to make
a move or at least show some envy.

I asked for time to think and rushed
head over heels to Paris. My family aghast:
you are ruining your last chance! Windham was
moody on arrival. "Not greeting me?"

"I was with the prisoners at the Tuileries.
First the workers wanted land and higher wages.
Now the king is locked up. One night he fled
to Austria, but when he paid the innkeeper

the man recognised him as the face on the coin
in his palm. All along the roads and streets
workers, row upon silent row, watching how
the sad coach passed back to the palace. Then
the city exploded in resinous hate with blood
streaming down the driveways to gelatinate

in stone seams. Some, can you believe it, who could
recite La Marseillaise were released!
Madame Lamballe, you remember her,
was led down a path paved with the corpses of all
her best friends accurately chosen by her servants.
The hairdresser got Madame's severed head to quickly rearrange

the wig before Marie Antoinette was made to kiss
her friend lifted on a pick-axe." "Only barbarians
can do such a thing!" "That's where you're wrong, Anne –
this is the amount of blood necessary to compel people
to see each other instead of each other's possessions."

"Dundas asked me to marry him."
He didn't look me in the eye.
He kept on talking –
for nearly four hours.

"I cannot decide…" (he said this dramatically)
"I can only give you up."

"Who marries whom he loves?"
"One marries respect, virtue, duty!"

"Beautiful as Apollo," said Lord Glenbervie of him last night
"but the man is irresolute down to his deepest soul."

"Why don't you just say:
because I, William Windham, do not love you?"

how dare I grieve here on the grape-dark journey
back   my body overcome with bereavement
my heart sluggishly silting up
afflicted with loss – a blue smallness I have to find
against growing old and other death-related
crunches as my fecund times have become

thin, brackish, croaking splinters –
dare I, while the revolution is the only valid word
while refugees dance in dresses flecked with blood
(a red ribbon indicates family members beheaded;
4000 already hacked to death) dare I, already
a pampered glutton, sit so utterly famished for love?

**given line: macho men give me the creeps**

given line: macho men give me the creeps
macho in the Afrikaans thesaurus: manly, as befits
a man, hardworking, valiant, brave
what is femininity? gracefulness, ruse,

handwork, soft, timorous, disgusted I page
with stiff forefinger to chauvinist: gushing
admirer of one's own people and fatherland
the dictionaries are boundary-obsessed

penis: manly rod
stick, cane, birch, for corporal punishment
dear god, what is the clitoris then?
rudimentary penis, never more, it says, therefore… therefore…

this sonnet is not a poet's odyssey, but a hermaphrodite's
attempted break-out of definition with steep nymphomaniac bleeps

## plea to be liberated

my poetry shines like an erstwhile whore
next to the slim-line mannequins of younger poets

but that's by the way

will liberty and brotherhood in the end prevent me
from being longlimbed lecherous   losing control over

a man's smell   exchanging might of deadly bow
to tender benedictory hip   not trying to write

the summer nearer with spun-out vowels but one
short-tempered voice one person telling you that I love

you   colostrumed in the colour of salmon and black metal –
iambically we should not let go of each other even on the sly

erstwhile piglets averse yet toothless not distressed that lines of struggle
sadly keep on felting in saffron – only the democratic enjambment

can soak the heart loose. oh beloved don't you see
behind all these words how desperately I fight

for liberation   so many syllables
I smite shut behind me so as to have it

at least once (I feel how you sink from me
and drive past the suburban poem

where you, bugger the struggle,
lavishly thrive with someone else)

## one day my husband feels I do indeed deserve

one day my husband feels I do indeed deserve
larger bookshelves of melamine

poetry volumes previously emotionally classified
now alphabetically please, he orders satisfied

with himself. DMP Botes's *What is an ordinary man first?* No,
thank god, with Boerneef Afrikaans poetry can burst on the scene

I go cold when I have to put TT Cloete's censorious fist
next to Breytenbach     our literature's only terrorist

nimbly but unalphabetically
I let Stephan Bouwer suffer as a buffer

Cussons lies like slices of bread
a woman living with the dead

then: oh, my classy heroine, the restrained Elisabeth Eybers
who collects the bitterest spaces with the iciest labours

Jonker and Krog dance hand on hip – young lovers blow by blow
begin reading poetry with us *en route* to the Louw-show in the next row

sturdy and strong the men hold their church with cosmic rites
where Opperman's *Komas* soared to unintelligible heights

he has to lie bodkin to licentious Stet
without murdering Koekie Ziervogel's wet-

ness    bitterly Small sneers smaller smalls Spies
next to them Stockenström peaks in Greek

Watermeyer could cut wheat in the highest class
but preferred to cymbal "volk" to Volkskas

my eye falls on a forgotten slim stack of Hambidge
she now lives between Eybers and me – as nouveau riche

## slaughtering cattle for the Dutch Reformed Church fête

bloodless robust carcasses kick
air on trestle tables    boer women in aprons
securely cut from fleshy buttresses

the light-coloured round biltong    steak
chuck    rib    the special "eye" biltong loosened from
its muscle basket    softly the string biltong

is torn from the bone    from embroideries of blubber
across silver sinews her knife nicks a bean-coloured gland
open like a rose    marrow bones lie knuckle-smooth

in meatier beds    Aunt Oubaas lets fall the T-bones
as regular as tiles from her sawing blade
oxtails marrow-eye from darkly smocked curly swirls of fat

arms flap cattle humps snailfoot flat on the wood
feed the guttural meatmill    soundlessly
from large bowls massive tongues lift

we rinse a nest of guts with lemons until it slips
open like condoms for sausagemeat: against the church hall
a reminder: All to the honour of the Lord

at the scale I stand my forehead wrinkled
to suspiciously name, weigh and price
to the honour or dishonour of God knows who

freezing the cost in ink.

## Lady Anne at the microwave oven

oh my Afrikaner sisters in kombis and station wagons
with stylish sunglasses and hair tinted against the grey
bodies that jog and gym and yoga in flowery leotards
                               fiercely clinging to pliancy and Pill

as we flit past one another on the highways
stop in dusty clouds next to sportfields
attentively gesticulate the rhythm outside music studios
pray one another to tears during Bible study
I am wondering: what kind of breed are we?

in the merciless methodology of planning
I recognise the insanity of packing an oxwagon
the passion with which children are pushed to excel
and persevere    smells of concentration camp and croup

and as we sit on sanderson linen and ooh and coo
and the men at the built-in bar drink desperately and talk about tits
we know that we are the last
the last whose children are being tenderly blonded on milk and honey
this is the end
behind us under us around us
with the soft sound of ash
structures that keep our kind in place
are crushing themselves to bits

## I smell him young behind the breadcutting machine

1

I smell him young behind the breadcutting machine
queue behind him boy with shiny
hair, skin rosy from afternoon school sport
"put it in" his fingers rumple the bag open

he pays for bread Car spins a condom packet
and my eyes become afflicted with
the qualities of his young skin
while I'm buying a wholewheat loaf Die Suid-Afrikaan and 4 Lucky Packets

2

at 35 my hair has left its sallow
for grey – fiercely
I leave the hairdresser
with a deadening dyed-brown array

3

from breastfeeding and the dodging
of bed manoeuvres we're now
on the road to middle age:
"Vasectomy?" I dare

"Sweetheart," says Cornelia
while her dream-nails glide
along the sofa piping
"I'd rather go without a chicken pen
than get into bed with flab-folia."

## ma will be late

that I come back to you
tired and without memory
that the kitchen door is open I

shuffle in with suitcases hurriedly bought presents
my family's distressed dreams
slink down the corridor the windows stained

with their abandoned language in the hard
bathroom light I brush my teeth
put a pill on my tongue: Thursday

that I walk past where my daughter sleeps
her sheet neatly folded beneath her chin
on the dressing table silkworms rear in gold

that I can pass my sons
frowning like fists against their pillows
their restless undertones bruise the room

that I can rummage a nightie from the drawer
slip into the dark slit behind your back
that the warmth flows across to me

makes me neither poet nor human
in the ambush of breath
I die into woman

## I will always remember

I will always remember the way you walked
in last night – you moved as if sparks
flew from you your eyes a mean
messy blue   then you held me as always

so that I had to raise my eyes to your secure mouth
your face determined your hands your neck your shoulders
cut under the impeccable shirt I smelled
on you the perfume of power   as your dark head

bent down to greet every child something
authoritarian stayed with your body as of one
who always lies on top your hands moved with
the orders of a boss   this morning I bring breakfast:

on the bedside table you put my monthly allowance – for the first
time I see how the word finance breathes the word violence

## strategically I do my best

1
strategically I do my best
the wheels crunch and
the cannon barrel shifts into the breach

2
the pelvis gets its familiar snap
knees easily fold their openness
even a slight slackness lets experienced lips smack

3
my days of fighting you are over.
I only want you preserved
as the one who remembers us

4
among the smoke and the slogan-shouting mouths
the accusations the violence the death in between
you belong nowhere you are the irrelevant wolverine

## ballad of the power game

in detail you keep tabs 1.1 your wife
1.2 other subjects 1.3 those in control
in the correct order you mention that we
2.1 continuously offend you 2.2 shrivel up from non-planning
2.3 even your simplest expectation we fail to live up to
this is no performance    your fury swoons and pain
of course we are all guilty darling    so even more you
have become man without power who measurelessly undermines

it is perhaps at this stage that you realise
in essence the marriage is over    all that governs
still is the social playing out of grievances and regret
love was the only and no factor. curtsey    reach    curtsey
always towards the household but the colour of crying
of bitter cradling in the oscillation of venom
as of now your self-image is no longer mine
woman without power who fruitlessly undermines

"because I married poorly!"
these words cross boundaries and can never
go back – a trust will have to take care of the retard after our deaths –
jesus but what is the defence?
– life gave me so much more!
due to your small terrain dear your enclosed domain
I proclaim your elegant assets    state your cynicism in honour
of a man without power who endlessly undermines

*l'envoi*
as offensively as fury dares to formulate
through the act of poetry: the subaltern – I don't feel
better    my wrists    palms wildly desire to overstep
words    to physically attack you as I would words

**illness**

the August wind blusters down the street
where I wait for the children in the car
a disconsolate haze hangs over the suburb
low dust fleeces the grass and fluttering daisies
I think of you in a high hospital bed
you have been for so long with me against me of me
I try to imagine you
loose
someone apart from me away from me from us
with difficulty I get you standing apart
loose and with the looseness
a fragility
as you must lie there
slender in your loosely striped pyjamas
and I think about how you are being overcome
more and more by this marriage
how surely the weight of it
burdens your thin wrists
how your heart – treacherous from stress –
like a tilting bird swerves behind your ribs

I think of your eyes when you greeted me
how like death they retreated how dry your tongue
how purulent the blister on your lip
what has become of you who are mine – suddenly
the school bell and our children
rearing against the wind so pale
so inclined towards each other so frail
so apart as if wind is all they know
you know you are all we have
that holds us together as if related

and I think of you
as of blood I think of you
while we drive on in silence
through this endless dismal August day

## Castle of Good Hope
## 14th Dec. – 1799

## Journal

For the ship anchoring to the side
I hastily prepare parcels and letters
– the coming and going of ships, high ranking officers'
movements lie like an umbilical cord to the Castle –
sweeping my eye across the bay has become second nature
and the thrill of locking my door and slowly mouthful by mouthful
tasting the post, the "latest" newspapers, letters
– the written word the only harbour
of the travelling heart.

Then the smell hits us – unearthly
so putrid it seems the most primordial
of stenches. It's coming from the bay
says the cook. By midday everyone knows:
a slave ship is unlawfully looking to put to land
609 Congolese – my husband suspects
the hold is under water, a few have drowned; rice, nuts
manioc finished. The obviously greedy upstart
captain of the ship implies that Governor Younge planned it all,
while he apparently hissed,
"Did you have to hang this maggots' nest
for all and sundry at the Cape to see?"

"But why does it smell so?" "Annie, in the ship,"
my stolid husband, "they are lying row upon row –
packed, shackled, to form filthy strings, shelf upon shelf.
The doctor does not dare go down because of diarrhoea,
heat, stench; the deck deadly slippery from mucus and blood."

I turn the dessert spoon over and over –
silver, expensively heavy, and catch myself
for days staring from every window
at the doomed ship in the bay.

At dusk a lament drifts towards the Castle,
a kind of howl, sobbing
from the abdomen of that pleading cargo of misery.
Through my telescope I see on the deck
shackled groups swaying to and fro in a macabre treaty
against death – a shoal of fins circling the ship,
waiting for the stiff tussle of bodies
cut loose every morning and thrown overboard.

After I had seen that
for many days my brain rushed forth
with a dim undetermined sense
of unknown modes of suffering.
In my thoughts was a darkness,
call it solitude,
a blank desertion,
no familiar shapes of trees,
of sea or sky, no colours of green fields
"But huge and mighty Forms that do not live
Like living men mov'd slowly through my mind
By day and were the trouble of my dreams"

– haunt me haunt me like a fever.

**Vineyard
14th May – 1800**

**To Henry Dundas**

Thus begins our new governor:
commission on every slave ship illegally dropping anchor
and the following "free blacks" executed this morning
for being "rebellious":

Domingo of Bengale
Moses Aaron of Makassar
Joost Ventura
Sampoernaij Abraham de Vyf
Rebe of Guinee
Jan Coridon
Mira Moor
Kijaija Moeda
and Claas Claasz of Bengale

Just a list of heretics
for future composers –

they hang this morning
on the open ground
next to the Castle:
a decorative marimba

# Journal

This sets loose so many images. From my earliest years
those without rights grinning from every landscape:

the slaves found to be unfaithful bound in bunches
by Telemachus, strung like doves in threads

so that their toes just-just touch the ground –
cruel nests. Through a noose all the heads are

plucked into the air; swinging they died, their eyes dry:
"their feet danced somewhat, but not for long."

Slave rebellions since the previous century in Barbados,
Guadeloupe, Jamaica and when I was ten

the revolt of Coromantine negroes in San Domingo –
the blood of whites and mulattos mixed with rum and tasted,

sugarcane farms burnt. I hear grownups speaking in codes:
rebels captured, feet in fires, anecdotes of the soundless

shining-eyed deaths, the name of origin like an ecstasy
on the tongue. Death becomes the only return, only escape.

Long thin shawl needles pushed into babies' brains,
break the tiny jaws after birth on plantations. Truly

only death takes you back to Africa. On our own estate
those in stone cottages on the cold thighs of Scotland

adopt the Lindsay surname, but furiously
groan Jacobin slogans in the pews.

And the widely quoted yell of Toussaint L'Ouverture
captured as a slave liberator: "By overthrowing me

you have only defeated the trunk of the tree of freedom;
it will grow back because its roots are deep, numerous

and vivacious – the threads of being free have been mercilessly
woven into every civilised tapestry's most intimate warp and woof."

Pronouncements like this fluster me into buying
a Wedgewood cameo necklace: am I not human *and* brother?

Refuse sugar with my tea, gather guilt and let me be
moved by Windham's anti-slavery campaigns:

>1. to belong to the privileged, deeply believing
>that the oppressed are inferior, will not be changed
>
>other than through an intense revolution
>2. to end slavery
>
>and commit ourselves to the most beautiful heroic poem
>in ourselves.   3. everything previously done, previously
>
>dreamt, hoped, sacrificed, previously bought at great cost
>is but a prelude to the impossible: to strip one another
>
>to brotherhood. (By the way: neither Windham nor Wilberforce
>are saddled with titles and treasures from the 11th century!)

# Journal

empty lies the interior of the land
next to the stony entrails of roads and pontoons
lie heaps of stones (slimy heaps of barracoons trail
        all the way to Woodstock beach)
as well as the white cysts of small villages
missionary stations like green gut-lining
the Gantouw and Amatola mountains slip kidney-purple from fatty clouds
empty lies the interior of the land

hesitant under the convex-concave gable
the families sit taciturn and divided in the gallery
the front door bolted against the interior
the howling of deceit and negotiations
briberies   we sit listening
to the lies of light and hoofs on the wet dark streets
every house besieged   every fact intercepted into rumours
in every bay it may now arrive:
treacherous rigging and hostile decks
empty lies the interior of this land

the categorical no means yes
industriously from its corrupt stomach drones the Castle
where officials make deals over sundowners and dinners
spit on lives in spittoons
life is abundant in this empty land

        and still on the mountains
        the fire and smoke remain
        the fire and smoke
        around the mountains' necks

a bizarre chalaza of loose coals like calabashes
from which fringes flame
empty lies the interior of the land

Vineyard
16th Feb. – 1801

**To Henry Dundas**

How many times do I want to write to you – long
silly letters, inappropriate, happy letters –
the whole Castle full of guests and song, yes
my head is full of you, dearest Dundas

but I have so many grievances that I want/
have to talk about: although thus promised,
my husband was not appointed as acting,
rather your nephew the stout Francis Dundas;

in the Castle he and Younge are now both living,
and we're kicked out to a cottage next to the Liesbeeck.
Mr Barnard remains swinging in the marionette cupboard –
not a single issue is discussed with him

and what issues they are! The Gardens
henceforth exclusively for the Governor's use;
the last of the funds are to be used for a *theatre*
and fishponds; to my dismay he even wants the staircase

*broadened* so his camarilla can parrot on their perch.
He is truly an unimpressive little runt, Dundas
who spends hours behind closed doors cheating
people out of their rights, personnel of perks.

Let me pull the lamp closer. It is late morning
but the mist and clouds drizzle in spittle
sounds from the lintels. From my window
the mountain is purely a surmise.

Shall I push my hand into the grey and grope
around until I can snatch it up, dry it lovingly,
polish the cliffs with my breath
and make it stand at my feet in the cold?

Dundas, the slaves work for gourds and blows,
the general rule is that of impunity, while bigmouth
men dance their boerdances to gavotte tunes!
Children order lackeys around and before I know it

I have opened my deepest hurt: we are
the subject of malicious gossip: Andrew is called
old goggle-eye, deflated chignon, I was, of course
your mistress, now a mere deposit, I hide illegitimate

children in London and yes even my sketches I have stolen
from Thibault (the HOIK's insidious architect). People say they see
me roam the streets – the Cape's own death banshee.
We are under surveillance, shunned, our post opened, so you see

dearest, it is so lonely here, wet and cold and wholly
wasted. My partner aloof, confused and warty
with reproach.... Adieu from this most southern quarter,
Your faithful friend, Anne Barnard

# Part III (end)

## January 1802

## Journal

Our hermitic vineyard cottage sold, belongings loaded yesterday
onto the Scarborough. Balder, with a resigned posture
of his neck that does not predict anything positive for future posts
I have to negotiate, Andrew stays behind for the Dutch takeover.
We took our leave of everybody; envying for the last time the neat
neighbourhoods, the streets
where nobody looks destitute, large rooms, full pantries and stores –
even in this heat deep cool roofs of oaks hold sway.

Andrew follows me everywhere with dog eyes. Why don't
we talk! I am more than aware of my wrinkles, my liver-spotted hands –
I so much OLDER – it seems he wants to say sorry
in advance, or, I could really not manage something for us,
or perhaps I am the best you could get,
while you are the only one I ever wanted to wed.
At breakfast the bailiff's call: boarding at 12 o'clock –
suddenly I'm overwhelmed with loss as I walk down under cannon shot.

Our Dutch friends wait on the beach visibly upset
as if they expect a disaster. Fare thee well, I mutter to the mountain:
may God protect this country from grief, never let
it be maimed by what freedom and power demand.
We row away in the small boat. On the ship
I lean over the rails, as under the salute everything
draws away from me: becomes smaller: the marrow
of slavery, tyranny, ignorance, seagulls hanging
in suspense; a continent as undiscovered fountain
of affirmation, its contours flowing with affectionate consent.

The sky with its windcleft clouds
darkens – the ship sails
with lanterns like tiny puddles
away into the night

## new alphabet

If you say A you must say B
A is always against apartheid
B is blind to colour

I want to write to you my brother but you are further away
than a woman in the previous century or even my country
of origin    as poem or document

if you say A you must say B
A is always against apartheid
B is blind to colour

so many guides leave me in the lurch
from so many sides I try approximately
to approximate you – the more garments I throw off
the colder it seems around me the further away you evidently are

if you say A you must say B
A is always against apartheid
B is blind to colour

my eyes don't get enough of thorn trees drowsy
among red grass and plovers with knitting needle-thin legs
my garden stained with cargoes of roses – only for my children
                                        will I lay down my life


here I learn to write – I can't do otherwise

**transparency of the sole**

the light over my desk
streams into darkness
I await my visitors on paper

my four children
finely balanced between anal and dorsal
tiny fins at the throat constantly stirring
eyes uncommonly soft
in the shallow brackish water your mother treads clay
with metaphors

come here across dictionaries and blank pages
how I love this delicate little school
these fish of mine in their four-strong flotilla
lured so close now what should I feed you?

dear child of the lean flank
yield to the seabed
yes the stretching makes you
ache but mother holds you to her mother
is here

the eye beneath like father's wondrous blue
migrates cautiously with a complex bunching
of nerve and muscle
till it's up beside the other
pert little mouth almost pulled out of shape
with time the tongue will settle in its groove
pigment of the upper flank begin to darken

unobtrusive between sand and stone you lie
meshed with bedrock never
again to prey or take flight
I press my mouth against each distended face mother knows

you will survive the tide

*(translated by Denis Hirson)*

## the heart is the toughest part of the body

*"The heart is the toughest part of the body.*
*Tenderness is in the hands."*

you say you already write on the screen of the electronic box –
while I am holding/folding/clawing with more than mere fingertips
the graphite point that stab-stabs from my handhollow
at the tough heart of the rose

**Lady Anne Barnard: remembered for her parties
in my history book**

daughter of the House of Lindsay
heroine with the thousand faces
this poem is our final showdown

woman for whom I've sharpened my blade for many years

naked (without possessions) next to your so-called pool
toenails yellowish   beautiful calves (brutally
I stare) sagging knees   the skin of your thighs

is old apple

your rusty breasts (in paintings
grotesquely bound) have areola and nipple
in one soft point because of no breastfeeding

(despite your drawing of a breastfeeding woman)

your weak abdomen I gather in my hand
it dissolves rennet-like into your fit vagina
gluey this big cream-coloured oyster

how close I am to you   my inhibitions set me free

nothing missing in this brief assault
except that you have become beautiful
to me and movingly brave

my head turns to search for your sound in the Castle

my cheek I hold against the dog roses
the steps   the water   like a wild shoot
your delicate nose blooms in a showcase downstairs

I bend to touch you overcome with tenderness

your barren hands rattle like reeds
you treated us always like an interesting park
but I look into your thin eyes

sparring blue even here next to your bath

only one life we have
in which we
want to be loved for ever

not opposite but together in this verse

lightfooted and without qualms the water
takes you into its lap I want to hold you
God I've become attached to your

soapy elbows crayoned in clever perspective

your neck stylishly turned somewhat bohemian
in the blonde shavings of your hair
distressed I mourn beloved friend

your complete utter radiant uselessness

"Kom, liewe reisgenote, laat ek u ter afsluiting 'n ikoon aanbied wat alles saamvat wat ek tot dusver met so 'n selfsugtige omhaal van woorde probeer sê het. Ons is nou hier op die agtste verdieping van UNISNOR, in Kamer 7, op 'n laaste Vrydag van die maand – skoonmaakdag. Van buite af moet dit byna lyk na 'n soort militêre maneuver as, op al die balkonne van die reusagtige gebou, die blou geuniformeerde swart vroue tegelykertyd verskyn met lappe en emmers, en vanaf die agterkant van die gebou oor die hele lengte na die voorkant beweeg, langsaam soos 'n oprukkende falanks van dekskroppers.

'n Mens sou by 'n filmopname van hierdie gebeure musiek van Wagner kon speel en dit verbeeld as die heroïek van die Nasionaal-Sosialistiese werkersklas. Maar van binne af, geraam deur die enkele vensterraam, is dit die onuitspreeklike lyding van 'n enkele vrou wat ons aanskou. Sy stap baie stadig en gelykmatig voor die venster verby met 'n lap in haar hand. Die willose hand-met-lap sleep voort oor die balustrade van die balkon – 'n gebaar wat meters voor en na haar verskyning in hierdie raam volgehou is. 'n Gebaar van gelatenheid tot die dood toe. Haar gesig soos 'n ghongplaat waarop 'n mens na gelaatstrekke soek, waarvan 'n mens uitdrukking verlang soos van 'n ghongslag – 'n soort ontlading. Maar die ontlading bly uit. Niks is hoorbaar behalwe die veraf gelykmatige gedruis van die verkeer op die snelweg vér onder nie.

Dan styg 'n straaljagter op van die militêre basis agter die Voortrekkerheuwel en skeur 'n perfekte boog om haar skouers verby, en laat 'n sidderende stralekrans van vlymende metale klank om haar kop. Sy toon geen belang. Dit is die dans van ons suster."

## a poem about guilt

1.

I want to write a poem that encompasses
all GUILT real and delusional

starting from: born in sin
i.e. with GUILT

up to going on trial
<u>in the name of</u> your neighbour

who doesn't care one iota about it
just tightens the yoke

<u>in the name of</u> the sweet-voiced ones:
there's no NEED to feel so GUILTY

<u>in the name of</u> house and hearth:
if you OWN much, you OWE much

<u>in the name of</u> Thus saith the Lord
who will not look:

GOD IS ON THEIR SIDE
who walk the roads
work with their hands
eat mostly bread and fish

"The Revolution,"
you never said,
"picked me clean"

debt only discharged
by BLOOD – mythic and mysterious

sacrifice SACRIFICE:
luxuries
and above all money
home detention
petitions and protest

but GUILT can also be how you get your kicks
a THERAPY against roaring distress

<u>in their name</u>: naturally also
GUILTY

<u>how many</u> and <u>who</u>
will give all of this BLOOD?


2.

in the beginning was the WORD
my next poem will say:
the one enigmatic word
that will hold in itself        no pasts just prophecies
                                    no mediators just mercy
                                    also everything
                                    that is blind blissful blood
in this destructive southeaster wind in Upper Mill Street
the poet wants to write a poem
beyond the burden of skeletons
of all who are lame and Afrikaans

but the tongue will have to lie differently:
free the most wordsome word through lines
that want to wingflap towards each other and in new ways
show the poem how
word becomes truth in this landscape
for the sake of the word alone
the new poem will have no end
bard who learns to listen

*(translated by Karen Press)*

**Gothic House
Wimbledon
1806**

(To William Windham – Secretary of War and Colonies.)

The 29-year-old Lord Caledon
is retaking control of the Cape.
You have appointed Barnard to accompany him temporarily.

Please Windham –
there is not money for both of us
to travel to the Cape. His health is poorly.
Is there not something

closer?


By return post:
BARNARD MIGHT TAKE THE APPOINTMENT OR LEAVE IT.
WILLIAM WINDHAM

## Wimbledon
## May 1807

Where will this letter find you best beloved?
If I could choose again
I would not have you return to the Cape.
May fair winds attend you and blow you back soon.

The six walnut seeds curved like tiny brains
burst their shells in the cotton wool.
I travel everywhere with the small gravure
of your face. At times your eyes look saddened

I think about you in the warm Cape
and memories of the mountain, the seven-foot people
percolate up and how I took all the wrong tubes
of watercolour. Oh, how I misjudged that brutal
and blissful light! Look after yourself.

Thank you for the loquat
which left two smooth
pips like teeth
in my mouth.

I miss you, my days
are ailing without you.

**Cape of Good Hope
June 1807**

I shudder
when I think
what space there is
between us.
Pray for me
sometimes, dearest love;
I never fail to do
so for you,

Andrew Barnard

## Cape of Good Hope
## August 1807

I will write
to my Anne
when I get back
from the hinterland.
May the Almighty
keep her
as always.

Ever her own,
Andrew Barnard

## Wimbledon
## November 1807

The six walnut trees in pots,
my hands dirty,
when the message came…

(But I had a letter yesterday!)
How can it be

how can it be
that that day passed over me
as if it was any other day?
that I sleep, have tea
laugh and potter,
while half of me
is already dead?

# Wimbledon
# 1808

Pawell brought me
a handful of relics:

* a locket with my hair

* the green purse I knitted for you

* your medicine

* of fever says the slave
  near Stellenbosch

* the doctor from the Cape was too late

* there was no-one with you

* you were buried on the road to Green Point
  a small funeral
  and wind from the sea

**neither family nor friends**

tonight everything speaks through the dead
towards me
your brittle bundle of bones
my longestloved beloved
lies lonely and longingly cradled somewhere lost
and lean
I am overwhelmingly awake tonight
of me so little has become
you are all I had in this world
beloved deathling
alone and cold it is behind my ribs
Africa had me giving up all
it is so dark
it is so bleak
soft beloved taunter
of me so little has become
I am down
to my last skin

# epitaph

Sacred to the Memory of
ANDREW BARNARD, Esq.
Colonial Secretary at the Cape of Good Hope
Departed this life the 27th October 1807.
Aged 45 years.

His afflicted widow who at a distance deplores her loss,
has erected this tablet as a mark of her liveliest sorrow.
Colonists! Drop a tear to his memory.
He sought the welfare of your country and he loved its
inhabitants.

**End**

I want to repeat the maxim of my father:
he who fails to closely examine
his life and his place in it
fails the Writer of his life.

My pen stepped into the breach for me
and recorded the time of roses and myrtle
until now where coldness
and silence lie along rows of cypresses.

This text has been patched together from diaries
and letters: not everything is true – I had
to lie and shorten a lot, but this way
it fits better among other texts that themselves
will speak to or reject in this wordweb.

## end

perhaps this ending should belong to me
(so many voices began talking in between)
should the poet survive rather than you Lady Anne?
besotted my hand wades along your neck into cascades of locks
who will ever know how "here" we were
who will note your petty flight and entrance who
chart your transformation who show confounded

what you participated in? not I says the Bard
I am the great exterminator! from title and trifle
I shall liberate us give us up and shout viva the sole!
(but as ever it depends on why we have come to this continent)
the epic heroine's destiny is directly linked to the bard's
can I ever change anything or even bend a boundary?
here men live from slogans alone

confused, longingly
I look towards singing into a new ending with you
apart from our miscalculations we have perhaps
been each other's conscience as well
but the most important part of this bankrupt poem
is its farewell to you (hear the gong at the gallows)
and your kind
and your kind's language
from now on you will have to dither elsewhere

under my thumb lies the delicate syntax of your throat.

# Sources

Barnard, Lady Anne. *South Africa a Century Ago. Letters Written from the Cape of Good Hope (1797-1801).* Edited with a Memoir and Brief Notes by W.H. Wilkins. London: Smith, Elder, & Co., 1901; 3rd ed. 1908.

Barnard, Lady Anne. *South Africa a Century Ago. Letters Written from the Cape of Good Hope (1797-1801).* Part I. Letters Written from the Cape of Good Hope. Part II. Extracts From a Journal. Selected and edited by H.J. Anderson; with an Introduction by A.C.G. Lloyd. Cape Town: Maskew Miller; Oxford: Basil Blackwell, 1924.

Barnard, Lady Anne. *The Letters of Lady Anne Barnard to Henry Dundas from the Cape and Elsewhere / 1793-1803 Together with her Journal of a Tour into the Interior and Certain Other Letters.* Ed. A.M. Lewin Robinson. Cape Town: A.A. Balkema, 1973.

Berryman, John. *Homage to Mistress Bradstreet.* New York: Farrar, Straus & Giroux, 1956.

Eliot, T.S. "What is a Classic?" in *On Poetry and Poets.* London and New York: Faber & Faber, 1957.

Fairbridge, Dorothy. *Lady Anne Barnard at the Cape of Good Hope 1797-1802.* Oxford: Clarendon Press, 1924.

Forché, Carolyn. *The Country Between Us.* New York: Harper Perennial, 1982.

Leatt, James, Theo Kneifel, and Klaus Nürnberger, eds. *Contending Ideologies in South Africa.* Cape Town: D. Philip, 1986.

Merchant, Paul. *The Epic.* London: Routledge Kegan & Paul, 1971.

Ovid. *Metamorphoses.* Translated by Frank Justus Miller. Revised by G. P. Goold. Loeb Classical Library 42. Cambridge, MA: Harvard University Press, 1916.

*Stet.* 3: 3 & 4. February 1986.

*Die Suid-Afrikaan.* February 13, 1988 & June/July 15, 1988.

*Upstream.* 6:1 Summer 1988 & 6:2, Autumn 1988.

Van Niekerk, Marlene. *'n Vlugskrif oor Feminisme* (np: 1987).

Watson, Stephen, *Selected Essays, 1980-1990.* Cape Town: Carrefour Press, 1990.

*Weekly Mail.* 4: 30, 5-11 August 1988.

Wordsworth, William. "The Prelude: Childhood and School-time." In *The Penguin Book of English Verse.* Edited by John Hayward. Harmondsworth: Viking Penguin, 1968.

# About the Poet

Antjie Krog's iconic status as one of South Africa's most popular and critically acclaimed poets began when she was eighteen with her first collection *Daughter of Jephta* (1970). In the decades since this explosive debut, Krog's many works – both poetry and prose – have received almost every award available in her country for poetry, translation and non-fiction, among them the esteemed Hertzog Prize for *Lady Anne* (1989), the Olive Schreiner Prize and the Alan Paton Prize for *Country of My Skull* (1998), and the Vita Poetry Award for *Down to my Last Skin* (2000). Internationally she has also been awarded the Stockholm Award from the Hiroshima Foundation for Peace and Culture as well as the Open Society Prize from the Central European University (previous winners of which were Jürgen Habermas and Vaclav Havel).

www.ingramcontent.com/pod-product-compliance
Lightning Source LLC
Chambersburg PA
CBHW031835230426
43669CB00009B/1360